5.12 12 10/10

Cowboy
Logic

Cowboy Logic

THE WIT AND WISDOM OF KINKY FRIEDMAN

(AND SOME OF HIS FRIENDS)

KINKY FRIEDMAN

ILLUSTRATIONS BY ACE REID

ST. MARTIN'S PRESS

New York

For Earl and Cabbie—
the cowboys of my childhood

*

BOOK DESIGN BY AMANDA DEWEY

Library of Congress Cataloging-in-Publication Data

Friedman, Kinky.
    Cowboy logic : the wit and wisdom of Kinky Friedman
(and some of his friends) / Kinky Friedman.
        p. cm.
    ISBN-13: 978-0-312-33156-6
    ISBN-10: 0-312-33156-8
    1. American wit and humor. I. Title.

PN6165.F76 2006
818'.5402—dc22

                                        2006041743

First Edition: May 2006

2   4   6   8   10   9   7   5   3   1

Contents

Acknowledgments

Many people have contributed their wit and wisdom to this book and to this life. For the sake of brevity, and to avoid ennui, I only mention those who've contributed in some way to this book. In a random and haphazard order, as my father would say, they are: Tom Friedman, Min Friedman, Billy Joe Shaver, Leon Dodson, Earl Buckelew, Kent Perkins, Willie Nelson, Marcie Friedman, Don Imus, John McCall, Sage Ferrero, Dylan Ferrero, Rita Jo Thompson, Captain Midnight, Tompall Glaser, Cousin Nancy Parker, Tony Simons, Roger Friedman, Max Swafford, Jimmie "Ratso" Silman, James Clare, Kristin Hedger, Madge Reid, Judge Gary Michael Block, Sammy Allred, Rev. Goat Carson, Ted Mann, Gov. Jesse Ventura, Dr. Jay Wise, and so many others that listing them would be tantamount to pissing up a rope.

I'd also like to thank David Vigliano and Elisa Petrini, my agents; Diane Reverand and Gina Scarpa at St. Martin's Press; and, finally, I'm sending eternal gratitude up to Hillbilly Heaven to the great Ace Reid.

Introduction

This book was fun to put together, ought to be fun to read, and hopefully, will be a financial pleasure. It may seem deceptively simple but I consider it to be one of the greatest literary achievements of my career. This is because it represents a lifetime of stealing other people's lines. That being as it may, I am proud to point out that nothing in this book has been *borrowed*. Even I would not sink that low.

A person who takes a simple idea and makes it tediously complex, we call an intellectual. A person who takes a tediously complex idea and makes it simple, we call an artist. But if you can condense the whole megillah into one line—then you really have something. In the history of civilization, the kings of the one-liners have been Oscar Wilde, Henny Youngman, Mark Twain, Will Rogers, and Colonel Travis at the Alamo, who drew one line in the sand, thereby creating the spiritual framework that one day would be Texas.

The green fuse that nurtures and sustains Texas, of course, is the cowboy. His humor, wisdom, and undying spirit pervade the land even as he vanishes from it. The art in this book is beautifully representative of the timeless dusty trail of the heart, bequeathed to us, the children of a troubled world, by the cowboy. It was created many years ago by the greatest cowboy cartoonist who ever lived, Ace Reid.

And finally, folks, this book will be published during my campaign for Texas governor, in which I'm trying to become the first Independent to win since Sam Houston in 1859. If I'm successful, and if you like this book, I'm afraid you're out of luck. I'll be working for the people of Texas and will have precious little time for future literary pursuits. If I lose, however, I have vowed to retire from politics in a petulant snit. During this time, rest assured, I shall continue to dump buckets of horse manure upon mankind for many years to come. I do not think I will lose, though. I *cannot* lose. The soul of Texas is riding on this campaign.

In the unlikely event that I do lose, however, weep not for the Kinkster. I always liked stray dogs better than fat cats.

1

COWBOY LOGIC

"I hate to be pessimistic, but I've seen some
bad droughts start out just like this!"

Happiness is a moving target.

We're not happy until
you're not happy.

If you're lookin' for a helpin' hand,
try the one on the end of your arm.

Never dig for treasure with
a short-handled shovel.

"Son, you'll never be a good cowboy unless you can
tell when one more piece of balin' wire
will break a shed down!"

If you can read this,
you're standing on my head.

—COWBOY'S EPITAPH

You can pick your friends and
you can pick your nose, but you
can't wipe your friends off
on your saddle.

It may not be the easy way,
but it's the cowboy way.

Anything worth cryin' can be smiled.

This country was a better place
when the cowboys all sang and
their horses were smart.

Everything comes out in the wash
if you use enough Tide.

Never take a whiz on an electric fence.

Be yourself—that way you never
have to remember who you are.

Courtesy is owed. Respect is earned.
Love is given.

If you want to wake up in the morning smilin', go to bed with a coat hanger in your mouth.

Anybody can drive a straight nail.

Only two kinds of people wear cowboy hats: cowboys and assholes.

The judges of who is a cowboy should be God and small children.

"You might think you're a cowboy, but them
critters ain't figured it out yet!"

It's okay to think you're a cowboy—
unless you happen to run into
someone who thinks he's an Indian.

Give a cowpoke enough rope
and he'll either hog-tie himself
or start up a rope factory.

Always seek wide open spaces,
except between your ears.

"The trouble with this big ole ranch is there
ain't anyplace to ever take a shortcut!"

Cheer up, it only gets worse.

Find what you like and let it kill you.

Hang on tight, spur hard,
and let 'er buck.

2

THINGS YOU WOULD NEVER HEAR A REAL TEXAN SAY

HE'D NEVER SAY:

I think that song needs more
French horn.

The tires on that truck are too big.

HE'D NEVER SAY:

I'll have the decaf latte, please.

Is that tuna dolphin-safe?

HE'D NEVER SAY:

I've got two cases of Perrier
for the Super Bowl.

William Robert, you appall me.

HE'D NEVER SAY:

There's no place in my home
for obscenity!

This red wine has a rather
cheeky bouquet.

HE'D NEVER SAY:

Duct tape won't fix that.

"He lost that eye while workin' on a ranch in the Panhandle. He left his spoon in his coffee cup."

HE'D NEVER SAY:

I believe the proper term is
"African American."

We don't keep firearms in this house.

HE'D NEVER SAY:

No kids in the back of the pickup;
it's just not safe.

Come to think of it,
I'll have a Heineken.

"Shore I wuz champion bulldogger at Madison Square
Garden in 1936. Help me lift my belly and I'll
show you my belt buckle!"

HE'D NEVER SAY:

Fried pig rinds are disgusting.

I thought Graceland was tacky.

HE'D NEVER SAY:

Will you go ahead with a home birth
if the baby arrives in Paris?

You're watching football? Change
the channel—Oprah is on!

" 'Course you ain't gonna see any football players,
you're watchin' the microwave!"

HE'D NEVER SAY:

Honey, I think we should sell the pickup and buy a family sedan.

You can't feed that to the dog!

HE'D NEVER SAY:

Wrestling is not real.

3

BLESSINGS,
CURSES,
AND OTHER
OBSERVATIONS ON
THE CONDITION OF
OUR CONDITION

**"Don't ask what kind of stick,
jist hand me a stick!"**

May the best of the past
be the worst of the future.

—FAVORITE IRISH TOAST

No matter where you go, sooner or later you see yourself in the rearview mirror.

The bathroom mirror is the perfect place to one day see the gypsy in your soul.

The only two good balls I ever hit
was when I stepped on the
garden rake.

Leap sideways, before your karma
runs over your dogma.

Where there's a will, there's a lawyer.

May all your juries be well hung.

—INSCRIPTION TO THE DEFENSE LAWYER
RICHARD "RACEHORSE" HAYNES

"Neighbor, it's plain to see why my cows are always
gittin' on yore place . . . you ain't keepin'
our fence fixed!"

A happy childhood is the worst
possible preparation for life.

If Mama Cass and Karen Carpenter
had only shared that ham sandwich,
they'd both be with us today.

A troubled mind will always declare
itself in a game of chess.

We knew with the true certainty of the arrogance of youth that we could have been anything, we could have done anything, except maybe get older.

I'm old enough to sleep alone.

Remember, Mr. President, we're not supporting their economy, we're burning their fields.

—UPON MY PRESENTING BILL CLINTON WITH A CUBAN CIGAR

The important things in life can never
be stolen; either they're already gone
or you haven't got them yet.

The important things in life
are not things.

"Mama, when I grow up,
I'm gonna be a musician."
"Make up your mind, son,
because you can't do both."

—LEGENDARY FIDDLE PLAYER
JOHNNY GIMBLE AND HIS MOTHER

I've never really cared much about what
people think, but I do care about
what they dream.

"Oh, I tried countin' sheep. I got to 5,000, sheared 'em, shipped 'em, and still lost money!"

A rationalization a day
keeps the shrink away.

Dreams can never hurt you.
Only the dreamer can.

JFK is not an airport, RFK is not a stadium, and Martin Luther King is not a street.

My father once said, "A man can be judged by the size of his enemies."

Fuck 'em if they can't take a joke.

—WILLIE NELSON

"Slim, is that one of them black widder spiders down
there close to your left hand, or am I seein' things?"

4

ALL POLITICS
IS YOKEL

You can lead a politician to water,
but you can't make him think.

I'm running for governor of Texas
because I need the closet space.

I don't know how many supporters I have, but they all carry guns.

I support gay marriage. I think they have every right to be just as miserable as the rest of us.

"Jake, if you'll vote fer me as County Commissioner,
I promise to fix your road jist like I did last election!"

"Yeah, she and I was hittin' it off fine, drinking beer
and holding hands, then I find out he's a
car salesman from California!"

I'm not pro-life. I'm not pro-choice.
I'm pro-football.

I'm running for governor—not God.

No teacher left behind.

"Awright, we got you fer stuffin' ballot boxes and
registerin' dead people—but I admire yore
interest in politics!"

I ask myself WWWRD:
What Would Will Rogers Do?

A fool and his money
are soon elected.

If you elect me the first Jewish governor of Texas, I'll reduce the speed limit to 54.95.

Trust me, I'm a Jew. I'll hire good people.

Criticize me all you want, but just don't circumcise me anymore.

—CAMPAIGN SLOGAN
SUGGESTED BY WILLIE NELSON

No lesbian left behind.

Politics is the only field in which
the more experience you have,
the worse you get.

The professionals gave us the *Titanic*;
the amateurs gave us the Ark.

Read my lips—I don't know.

George W.'s a good man trapped
in a Republican's body.

Jesse Ventura just didn't realize that wrestling is real and politics is fixed.

I believe musicians can run this state better than politicians. We just won't get a lot done in the mornings.

I'll fight wussification if I've got to
do it one wuss at a time.

I'm for the little fellers—not
the Rockefellers.

Davy Crockett didn't die at the
Alamo so we could have a choice
between paper or plastic.

The Democrats and the Republicans
have become the same guy admiring
himself in the mirror.

I'm going to lower the drinking age to eighteen. If you're old enough to die in Iraq, you're old enough to drink.

It takes a real dumbass not to understand the value of an education.

I'm going to bring back the Ten
Commandments to the public schools.
I may just have to change their
name to the Ten Suggestions.

I'll keep us out of war with Oklahoma.

I've got a head of hair better than Governor Rick Perry's. It's just not in a place I can show you.

I can't screw things up any worse than they already are.

"There they go again—always arguing if it's the
Republicans or the Democrats that won't let it rain."

Never reelect anybody.

5

KINKY
ON KINKY

Today I have millions of fans,
many of whom are attached
to the ceiling.

Friedman's just another word
for nothing left to lose.

One of these days they're going
to make a life out of my movie.

When your whole life's a vacation,
it's tough to decide when to leave.

"It's worth a trip to foller this guy jest to see
what he does when he gits where he's goin'!"

I'm the oldest living Jew in Texas
who doesn't own any real estate.

I'm a giver in a taker's body.

I mostly ride two-legged animals.

I mourn the passing of
Thousand Island dressing.

I piss on Hollywood. I piss on the *New York Times* Bestseller List. Sometimes, like Van Gogh, Hank Williams, and Charles Bukowski, I even piss on myself.

If you look deeply enough into yourself, you'll soon discover you can see everybody else.

"What's the matter with you? Haven't you
ever seen a real cowboy?"

The only secrets I've kept
are the ones I've forgotten.

I drive a Yom Kippur Clipper.
That's a Jewish Cadillac. It stops
on a dime and picks it up.

Either I'm not a practicing Jew or else
I've got to practice a little bit more.

I was born in Chicago, lived there one year, couldn't find work, and moved to Texas, where I haven't worked since.

I'm sixty-one, but I read at the sixty-three-year-old level.

I'm not afraid to live. I'm not afraid
to die. I'm not afraid of success.
I'm not afraid of failure. I'm not afraid
to fall in love. I'm just afraid I may
have to stop talking about
myself for five minutes.

When I meet someone I'm usually good for about three minutes of superficial charm. After five minutes, I can often see the pity in their eyes.

I've always been searching for a lifestyle that doesn't require my presence.

Every time I stay at a fancy hotel, some
employee always comes up to me with
deep suspicion in his eyes and says,
"Can I help you?"

I am a dreamer who never sleeps.

—ATTRIBUTED TO MY LATE FRIEND
CAPTAIN MIDNITE

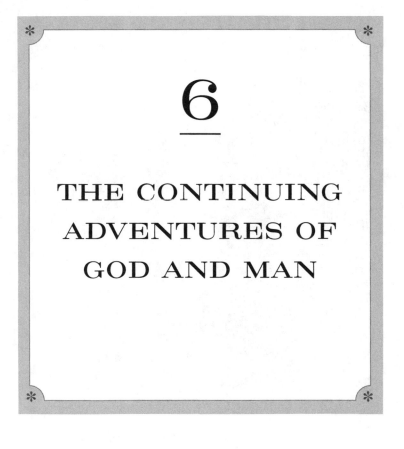

6

THE CONTINUING ADVENTURES OF GOD AND MAN

"It's good to see you back. What is it this time?
A drought or a break in the cattle market?"

If you don't love Jesus, go to hell.

—THE WORDS OF MY SPIRITUAL ADVISER,
BILLY JOE SHAVER

Wash your hands and say your
prayers, 'cause germs and
Jesus are everywhere.

If Moses had been a committee, the Jews would never have gotten out of Egypt.

—TOM FRIEDMAN

They ain't makin' Jews
like Jesus anymore.

The only thing wrong with Southern
Baptists is that they don't hold 'em
under long enough.

—HEARD IT FROM A METHODIST

The downside to being an atheist is that
when you die your tombstone will
probably read: All dressed up
and no place to go.

I'd probably be a Buddhist,
if it weren't for Richard Gere.

I believe that Willie Nelson
is the hillbilly Dalai Lama.

I'm a Judeo-Christian with Jesus and Moses in my heart—two good Jewish boys who got in trouble with the government.

A lot of folks died in the Bible, but a hell of a lot more died because of it.

The Old Testament tells us that in
six days the Lord created the heavens
and the earth and all the wonders therein.
There are those of us who feel He might
have taken just a little more time.

5-7

"God said he wasn't makin' any more land! Wul, if he
messed up on the rest of it like he did this,
I don't blame him!"

If you've seen one Sistine Chapel,
you've seen them all.

The people who survived the Crusades,
the Inquisition, and the Holocaust just
want a good table in a restaurant.

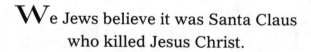

We Jews believe it was Santa Claus
who killed Jesus Christ.

As we grow older our picture of God becomes faded, coffee-stained, and fuzzier, and maybe we start to carry it in our wallets instead of our hearts.

The greatest sermons are not delivered—they are lived.

"Jake, I came out here to talk to you about the church, but after havin' to open and close all your gates, I've lost my religion too!"

May the God of your choice bless you.

7

TREASURES
AND
PLEASURES

"Man, this is better'n bein' rich. Jist owe everybody
so much they gotta be nice to you."

Every journey of a thousand miles
begins with a cash advance.

Imagination is the money of childhood.

Every time my friend Pat Green leaves a bar, he always asks himself the same question: "Can I puke in a straight line?"

Beauty is in the eye of the beer holder.

Never drink downriver from the herd.

Guinness: the drink that kept the Irish
from taking over the world.

When our accountant, Danny Powell, once asked my father what his financial goals were, Tom replied, "My financial goals are for my last check to bounce."

Thanks! It's been a financial pleasure.

A gypsy's definition of a millionaire is not a man who has a million dollars but a man who's spent a million dollars.

**"Those people who ride horses fer fun
never had to ride 'em for work!"**

I was so high I needed a stepladder to scratch my ass.

We Jews have had cocaine around for thousands of years. We just always called it horseradish.

The only currency I value
is the coin of the spirit.

Even my autographs are bouncing.

I smoke as many as twelve cigars a day, and I expect to live forever. Of course, I don't inhale. I just blow smoke at small children, vegetarians, and anybody who happens to be jogging by.

In order to effectively determine guilt or innocence, juries should be empaneled entirely from a population of prostitutes, bartenders, and bellmen from sleazy hotels.

I've been in outhouses, whorehouses, and White Houses, but I was proud to say I'd never darkened the door of a spa.

I was drunk enough to go
duck hunting with a rake.

Whether or not the bottle is half full
or half empty depends upon whether
or not you are half full of shit.

Native Americans believe you can't really own land, a horse, or a waterfall. The only thing they believe you can really own is a casino.

8

ADVICE TO PEOPLE WHO ARE HAPPIER THAN I AM

Never eat a sandwich bigger
than your head.

You're born alone and you die alone,
so you might as well get used to it.

"Yep, Jake, it looks hopeless,
but I don't think it's serious!"

Let Saigons be bygones.

Ballet is basketball for homosexuals.

Never say "fuck"
in front of a c-h-i-l-d.

I've always possessed the two qualities that Ingrid Bergman claimed were essential to happiness: good health and a bad memory. At least I *think* it was Ingrid Bergman.

The only things we ever keep are the things we let slip between our fingers.

"Jake, I shore admire you—with all these hard times,
and you seem so happy and unconcerned!"

I've always believed that people who laugh loudly in restaurants are usually not very happy.

You never know what the monkey eat until the monkey shit.

Treat children like adults
and adults like children.

Always respect your superiors,
if you have any.

Man's ability to delude himself
is infinite.

Balls, like imagination,
seem to shrivel with age.

Life is short;
Italian salamis are long.

9

THE GREAT
STATE OF TEXAS

"Jerk the backstrap, cut the hams into steaks, the rest into chili, and have the head mounted!"

I'm proud to be an asshole from El Paso.

In Texas, remember: "y'all" is singular,
"all y'all" is plural, and "all y'all's"
is plural possessive.

It's no disgrace to come from Texas. It's just a disgrace to have to come back.

In Texas, the men are men
and the emus are nervous.

I miss the days when cowboy shirts never had buttons and coffee with a friend was still a dime.

Texas may not be the Left Bank of Paris,
but how many different kinds of sauces
can you put on a chicken-fried steak?

In Texas, it's all Coke
unless it's Dr Pepper.

"Look at *yeeeew!*"
"No, look at *yeeeeew!*"

—TWO WOMEN GREETING
EACH OTHER IN TEXAS

The difference between Texas and New York is the difference between horse shit and pigeon shit.

In Texas we consider anyone a queer who likes girls more than football.

"No, it ain't always terrible hot here. Sometimes it's
miserable windy or unbearable cold!"

Said the Texan to the Yankee,
"All this land is good for is to hold
the world together."

If you've spent any time in the Lone Star
State you've no doubt seen, or possibly
even interacted with, the female creature
known as the Texas Big Hair.

As our first female governor,
Ma Ferguson, said "If English was
good enough for Jesus Christ,
it's good enough for Texas."

The rebirth of the human spirit can occur in the most unlikely places, such as motels, men's rooms, mental hospitals—in fact almost anywhere other than the Jewish Singles of Dallas Purim Party.

Hell yes I'm a real Texan! I have affidavits from twenty-five hundred sheep!

If you hear a Texan exclaim, "Hey, y'all, watch this!", stay out of his way. These are likely the last words he will ever say.

" 'Ole hoss, I just don't know who's the biggest fool—
her fer jumpin', or us fer holding onto her."

In Texas we believe that duct tape
can fix a broken heart.

I'm married to Texas.

In Texas we all share the common religious belief that if we live a good life, when we die we go to Willie Nelson's house.

"Hey, Jake, how about your coffee break?"

10

LOVE, MARRIAGE, AND OTHER HOPELESS CAUSES

If there's one thing I know about true love, it is that sooner or later it results in a hostage situation.

Can you call me back? I'm right in the middle of someone.

Get your biscuits in the oven
and your buns in the bed.

The couple did not need a marriage
counselor, they needed a taxidermist.

"What do you mean you think the magic
has gone out of our marriage?"

A blow job given with love is as beautiful as dogs playing poker.

If people said what's really on their
minds during sex, this would be
a world of one-night stands.

In the sky of every love affair are
little tickets to hell, falling like
confetti from the stars.

I could imagine a number of things that would've looked good on her. One of them was myself.

Women are like taxicabs. If you pursue them with great ardor, you'll never have them.

The main health hazard in the world today is people who don't love themselves.

There's no reason to let little things put a strain on a relationship that's already hanging by spit.

"Maw, I love you because you're gorgeous,
sexy, and a heck of a gate opener!"

The Southern gentleman's approach rarely cuts much ice with a lesbian.

What we once thought of as refreshing takes only a little time to become quite tedious.

Condoms may save you from AIDS,
but they can't save you from the more
deadly diseases we sometimes
refer to as life and love.

I can make my own sandwich.

Time is the money of love.

You never marry the person you
first see *Casablanca* with.

Jewish divorces are always the most
expensive. That's because
they're worth it.

There is a place where you
can go
Where Marilyn's still dancin'
with DiMaggio
And Juliet, with Romeo,
And the name of the place
is love.

"Oh Jake, the only thing that could be purtier than
to-nite would be a slow three-day rain."

11

WRITING
FOR FUN
AND PROPHET

There's a fine line between fiction
and nonfiction, and I believe I
snorted it in 1976.

The art of writing fiction is to sail as
dangerously close to the truth as possible
without sinking the ship.

"Paw, I don't think I'll ever finish this novel about
my life as a ranch wife. My tears keep rustin'
up the typewriter!"

This is the twenty-fourth book that I've churned out—I mean, carefully crafted.

Publishing four books in one year is an index of the emptiness of your life.

Talent is its own reward. If you have it, don't expect anything else.

True greatness is usually determined by Japanese insurance companies.

Every story has an end, and every friend has to go back to California.

Only write for those who can read between the lines.

"And with the roar of a .45, Cactus clutched his bloody
chest and fell facedown in the dirt."

Every artist should be ahead of his time
and behind in his rent.

An editor is a person who takes something great and makes it good.

Success in your own lifetime is the kiss of death for immortality.

I happen to have a large penis like Ernest Hemingway, not a small penis like F. Scott Fitzgerald. Now the only matter I still have to settle is whether I want to blow my fucking brains out or merely drink myself to death.

If you've written one book, you've written one book. If you've written two books, you're an author. If you've written more than twenty books, of course, you're a hack.

One good aspect of being mediocre is that you're always at the top of your game.

Great art is rarely performed with conscious intent; it is accomplished quite accidently by a death-bound passenger of life who is burning the candle at both its ends, ostensibly to avoid paying the electric bill.

Writing a novel is like Frisbeeing your soul into hell and hoping that some three-headed, flatulent dog might catch it.

If you like the book, never meet the author.

My life is a work of fiction.

"Hey, Jake! It says here, 'Cowboys have a
glamorous and excitin' life.'"

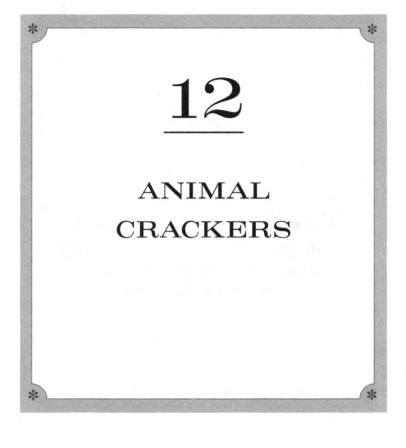

12

ANIMAL
CRACKERS

The neighbors asked my friend Slim why his cats were always going into their garbage cans. He told them, "They wants to see the world."

Money may buy you a fine dog, but only love can make him wag his tail.

The cat, of course, said nothing.

"Hey! Where you goin' with my dog!"

Somewhere, said John D. MacDonald, there is a planet inhabited principally by sentient armadillos who occasionally carve up dead humans and sell them as baskets by the roadside.

Dogs are cowboys; cats are Indians. Like the yin and yang of our souls, they fight across the dusty plains of childhood, their only fault, that they don't live long enough.

**"Boy it's hot when you see a dog chasin' a rabbit
and they're both walkin'!"**

When the horse dies, get off.

Justice rides a slow horse,
but it always overtakes.

Nothing in life is sadder than
a lobster tank.

Kill a spider, kill your dreams.

I have always felt that what we do when a stray spirit crosses our path—how we react to the hungry, homeless stranger— is indubitably a measure of our own humanity.

Unlike women, childhood, and various
other lost opportunities in life, cats
usually come back from wherever
it is they go.

If you see a sad man,
he'll have a sad dog.

I believe when you die and go to heaven, all the dogs and cats you've ever had in your life will come running to meet you.

"Yep, this is my watchdog—he watched them steal
my trailer, saddle, blanket, bridle, and fifty
pounds of oats!"